Everything You Need to Know About

SELF-CONFIDENCE

Feeling unsure of yourself is a sign of low self-confidence.

Everything You Need to Know About
SELF-
CONFIDENCE

Matthew Ignoffo, Ph.D.

THE ROSEN PUBLISHING GROUP, INC.
NEW YORK

Published in 1996 by The Rosen Publishing Group, Inc.
29 East 21st Street, New York, New York 10010

First Edition

Manufactured in the United States of America.

Library of Congress Cataloging-in-Publication Data

Ignoffo, Matthew.
    Everything you need to know about self-confidence / Matthew
Ignoffo. — 1st ed.
        p.   cm. — (The need to know library)
    Includes bibliographical references and index.
    Summary: Suggests how self-confidence can be built and describes
the positive effects it can have.
    ISBN 0-8239-2149-2
    1. Self-confidence—Juvenile literature.   [1. Self-confidence.]
    I. Title. II. Series.
    BF575.S39I46   1995
    158'.1—dc20   95-8758
                                                                         CIP
                                                                         AC

Contents

Introduction

Here's a quick quiz:

1. Do you believe in yourself?
2. Do you think you can do the things that you want to do?
3. Do you think other people do better than you because you're not good enough?

If you answered no to 1 and 2 and yes to 3, you probably lack self-confidence. That's the bad news.

The good news is that you're definitely not alone. Most people have some form of low self-confidence, no matter how confident they seem.

There's even better news. This book will tell you how to let go of your doubts about yourself and how to build your confidence.

Lack of confidence is usually described by words like "shy," "frightened," or "timid." They refer to a basic distrust of yourself that makes you hold back from doing everything you could do and being all you could be.

"Confidence" means faith in yourself. We may lack faith in ourselves because we've had bad

People who are described as shy, frightened, or timid are often people with a lack of self-confidence.

experiences and we've been told things like, "You're no good," "You really goofed up," and "You can't ever do anything right!"

After a while, we begin to talk to ourselves the same way. We call ourselves "Dummy" or "Fool," and we say, "I'm just no good at this." We begin to expect bad things to happen, and when they do we tell ourselves, "I knew that would happen."

Suppose a strong wooden plank is lying on the ground. The plank is six feet long, one foot wide, and two inches thick. I could easily walk from one end of the plank to the other. But imagine that this same plank is placed between the tops of two ten-story buildings. What would happen if I tried to cross the plank now?

Self-confidence is very much a state of mind.

In my head I would probably be saying, "That's a long way to fall. If I fall, I'll get killed. I hope I don't fall."

I'd either refuse to cross the plank or I'd probably fall—even though crossing that same plank was no problem when it was on the ground. What does the plank have to do with you and your confidence? You'll see as you read this book.

Everyone feels self-doubt at some point in their lives.

Chapter 1

Learning About Confidence

Actors, astronauts, and Olympic athletes sometimes experience loss of confidence. You're not alone. In fact, you're in pretty good company.

Low self-confidence can actually serve a purpose. Knowing this purpose will help you understand how to improve your confidence.

The Purpose of Low Self-Confidence

Poor self-confidence provides a risk-free "comfort zone" where you can hide. You won't feel comfortable in this "comfort" zone, but at least you won't risk anything by staying here. This "comfort" seems easier than working at improving yourself. But you actually use up more energy staying where you are than you would use by developing your talents.

Malcolm has just arrived in a new school. He

has played basketball very well for several years, but now at the tryouts he starts to sweat and feels his legs shaking. He tells himself, "If I mess up here, everyone will think I'm just a big jerk." He paces back and forth nervously.

He might go out on the court and throw some super shots. But more likely, either he will be so anxious that he'll do as poorly as he expects to do, or he'll decide not to try out at all.

By doubting himself, Malcolm remains a new student that nobody knows. He tells himself, "I'm no better off, but I'm no worse off either." He isn't happy, but at least he has risked nothing. He feels secure.

Staying in your comfort zone robs you of your potential. The false security starts to run your life, and eventually it can ruin your life. It keeps you from becoming who you really are. Being confident is having faith in who you really are.

How Confidence Works: Self-Talk

Poor self-confidence is manufactured. It is not your fate, even though you may think it is.

People manufacture self-confidence by using self-talk. Self-talk is simply what you tell yourself. You talk to yourself all the time, either in words or feelings. You may feel happy or depressed. You may think, "This is really cool!" or "This is

The brain is like a computer. A positive "program"—self-talk—yields positive results.

terrible!" You might say, "Great!" or "Bummer!" All of these reactions are forms of self-talk.

As he waited to try out for the basketball team, Malcolm told himself, "Everybody will think I'm a jerk." Focusing on that thought, he became less confident. His self-talk was so powerful that he would either do badly or not even try. Yet he has been a good basketball player for years.

What You Think Is What You Do

A computer runs whatever program you put into it. The same thing happens in your brain. Computer people say, "GIGO": GARBAGE IN, GARBAGE

13

Low self-confidence can prevent you from trying anything new.

OUT. If you put good information in, you get good information out. What you are thinking is the program that influences what you do.

Annette has to learn a part for the school play, but she tells herself, "It's too many lines to learn. I don't know how I'll be able to say all these speeches in front of an audience. I'll freeze on stage." Annette puts this negative self-talk into her mental computer. Then she has difficulty learning the lines and feels scared every time she thinks of being in front of the audience.

This process happens not because she can't learn the lines, but because she is manufacturing her own defeat.

Annette is making a mental image of herself as

a person who can't learn lines and has stage fright. The picture in her mind will always be reflected in what she thinks and does. Likewise, what she thinks and does will always be reflected in her mental self-image.

By not risking the basketball tryout, and by avoiding going on stage, Malcolm and Annette are "playing it safe." They are wearing their self-image for protection and security.

But by being afraid to risk something new, they both get stuck where they are. They can't grow into the people they could become. Malcolm never tries out. Annette freezes up on stage. Now they have their **results**. They talk to themselves about the results, put that information into their computer programs, and go through the cycle again.

The Self-Fulfilling Prophecy

A common statement is, "I knew that would happen." This kind of self-talk is called the self-fulfilling prophecy. It means that what we expect to happen will happen, not because it is our fate, but because we manufactured the results we expected.

The self-fulfilling prophecy works either for you or against you, depending on what you expect of yourself. You can put either a good program or a bad program into your mental computer. It depends on what you tell yourself and how you picture yourself. Remember: You change your confidence by changing your thoughts.

Chapter 2

Thinking Is Connected to Confidence

Some caution is good since it prevents us from walking off cliffs or into fires. But when caution controls you too much, you stop growing. Push back your protective mental walls to be more of who you can be. The walls are there to protect you from harm, but unless you expand the space within the walls, you stop living and become like a programmed robot.

Erroneous Thinking

We all want to avoid making mistakes. To do so, our instinct is to be cautious and follow the rules rather than being creative. But suppose a baby learning to walk tried to protect itself that way?

Fortunately, the baby doesn't use negative self-talk. The baby keeps getting up on two feet, falling down, getting up, falling down, getting up, and

People with low self-confidence often don't trust their own ability to make effective decisions.

finally taking a first step. Like the baby, at some point we have to let go of our fears.

The Poor-Confidence Cycle

You manufacture low self-confidence when you get caught in the cycle of negative self-talk. This cycle has nothing to do with things, people, or events outside of you. It has everything to do with the way you think about those things, people, or events.

There are seven types of negative self-talk that create poor self-confidence.

Perfectionism. If you think you have to be perfect to be acceptable, you'll never be acceptable because you'll never be perfect.

Jamal's self-talk goes like this: "I'll never be good enough to get a date with Tanisha. She wants a guy with lots of money to spend on her. She'd never even talk to me."

Tanisha is telling herself, "Jamal is so cool. It would be great to go out with him, but he'd never ask me."

Both Jamal and Tanisha are caught in the trap. They are using "all or nothing" self-talk: "Either I'm perfect or I'm a failure." They stop themselves from talking to each other because of perfectionism.

If you were really perfect, life would be very boring. There would be nothing for you to learn or create. Be glad you aren't perfect.

Judgmental Thinking. We make negative judgments about ourselves and other people. We set such high standards that nobody can measure up to them.

Pedro would like to play the piano, but every time he practices he tells himself, "You're off the beat, stupid!" When he listens to the other band members playing, he thinks, "What a bunch of losers! We'll never play well enough to perform."

Negative judgments about ourselves and others alienate us from ourselves and even from people who might help us. As a result, we feel lonely, and loneliness makes low self-confidence worse.

Many people turn to food when they feel lonely or hopeless. Food doesn't make the problem or the feelings go away, but changing your self-talk to include positive statements can help you gain the self-confidence you need to deal with the problem head-on.

Helplessness and Hopelessness. In psychology this kind of thinking is called "external control." We see ourselves as being controlled by parents, teachers, friends, society, and life. We feel helpless and see our situation as hopeless.

Barb is ashamed because she is overweight. She tells herself, "My parents are overweight, so I inherited my fat. When I go out, I'm supposed to eat a lot just to be friendly. People would laugh if I took up jogging. I wish I could lose this fat, but I can't."

This thinking often takes the form of "I wish I could, but . . ." By indulging in it, you lock yourself into a prison of your own making.

Impoverished Thinking. We tell ourselves that we'd feel better if we had something that is missing in our lives.

Angela thinks, "If only I had a stereo system like Annette's, everything would be great. If only I had a hairstyle like Barb's, I'd look fine. If only I had a body like Kandace's, the guys would be attracted to me."

"If only" thinking doesn't work. Things outside of ourselves cannot make us confident. Confidence comes from within.

Worry. We think that if we worry enough, it will somehow help.

Nathon is running for president of his club. He is preparing a campaign speech. He thinks, "What if the microphone doesn't work? What if the room is too hot? What if I forget what I want to say?"

Worry involves the "What if?" trap. We imagine everything that could go wrong. Nathon thinks that by worrying he is preparing for the speech. Actually he is making himself more nervous.

Victim Thinking. When we don't face reality and take responsibility for our reality, we see ourselves as victims.

Kandace is considered the most attractive woman in her office. She tells herself, "The guys all think of me as a sex object, and the women are jealous of me. I wish I weren't good-looking. I hate being afraid of my own body."

Victim thinking causes us to see reality as

Material things like clothes and hairstyles alone can't make us feel confident.

beyond our control. We feel we cannot take any responsibility for what happens to us. Pushed to the extreme, this kind of thinking causes us to hate ourselves because we seem so weak.

Self-Fulfilling Prophecy. The self-fulfilling prophecy was mentioned in Chapter 1. This kind of thinking comes from the other six types of erroneous beliefs. Notice how Jamal, Tanisha, Barb, Pedro, Angela, Nathon, and Kandace are setting themselves up to fail. They lack confidence simply because of the way they think about themselves and the world around them.

Thinking negatively about yourself may actually cause you to fail at what you're trying to do.

Recognizing the Low Self-Confidence Trap

The first step in changing yourself is to be aware of these erroneous beliefs. You have to know what the problem is before you can do anything about it. Becoming aware of what you are doing to yourself is the first step. You can build your new confidence by avoiding the negative self-talk trap.

Self-talk is like a powerful drug. It can be a harmful narcotic that destroys you and your life, or it can be penicillin that heals you and helps make you stronger.

The Power of Choice

People who have lost confidence in themselves usually believe in luck. Relying on luck to solve your problems relieves you of any sense of responsibility. But as soon as you begin to take responsibility for what happens in your life, you begin to see that things you used to attribute to luck actually are the result of choices you make.

Make the decision now to change your life by changing the way you think about yourself. This moment of decision gives you the power of choice—your choice.

Chapter 3

Knowing Yourself

To have confidence in yourself, you must know who you are and how you work.

Your Needs

Dr. William Glasser has helped many people understand themselves better so that they can create better behavior. Dr. Glasser believes that we have four needs:

The Need to Belong. We join clubs, have friends, and express our love and our desire to be loved. If we feel that we belong to nothing, love no one, and cannot find love, we are very lonely. Loneliness destroys confidence.

Malcolm felt so unsure of himself that he decided not to try out for the basketball team. He felt a need to belong to the team, but his self-defeating thoughts kept him from fulfilling his need.

Joining a club or a sports team or getting a part-time job may help improve your self-confidence.

Jamal and Tanisha wanted to go out together, but they were both afraid of rejection. They felt the need to love and be loved, but their self-limiting beliefs stopped them from expressing their feelings to each other.

The Need to Achieve. Confidence exists only when we can accomplish something we think is worthwhile. If there is nothing we feel we can do well, we view ourselves as weak. We think that there is no purpose to our lives.

Annette wanted to be in the school play, but she was so worried about forgetting her lines that she did badly in rehearsals. She felt her need to achieve, but she kept sabotaging herself.

Pedro wanted to play the piano with the band, but he was so critical of himself and the others that he undermined his own talent. He felt the need to demonstrate his skill, but his self-talk held him back.

The Need for Fun. Fun comes from having something to look forward to. If we can't look forward to a better future, we feel that our lives are going nowhere.

Angela thought her life would be better if she had new material things. But she did nothing to change her view of herself, and so she remained frustrated. She felt the need for fun, but her self-defeating views stopped her from making fun happen.

Malcolm was trying to fulfill the need for fun by playing basketball. Pedro was looking for fun by playing the piano. Jamal and Tanisha were looking for the fun they might have by getting acquainted. But all of them limited themselves by staying inside their mental prisons.

The Need for Freedom. We need to see ourselves as independent human beings. If we think we are victims of circumstances beyond our control, we lose the will to live. If we no longer feel alive, we slowly die.

Barb wanted to lose weight to avoid feeling like a slave to what she thought was inherited fatness. Even though she felt the need for freedom, she stopped short of fulfilling it by viewing herself as unable to eat sensibly and exercise.

Part of being free is recognizing that you are responsible for making your own decisions.

On the other hand, Kandace is very attractive, but she thought that men viewed her only as a sex object and that women were jealous of her. She felt the need to be free of other people's thoughts, but she did not realize that those thoughts really had no power over her. It is her own thoughts that have power over her, and she has not yet learned to control them.

Malcolm, Jamal, Tanisha, Barb, Pedro, Angela, Nathon, and Kandace are not aware of their needs. Therefore they have no idea that their lack of confidence stems from the fact that they are not actively fulfilling those needs. Once you are aware of your needs, you can keep growing.

Chapter 4

Making Your New Plan

If you don't know where you are going, you'll end up someplace else.

Goals

There is an old saying, "No wind favors a ship without a destination." Imagine a ship in the middle of the ocean. If the ship has nowhere to go, the crew can't set the sails to make use of any wind. The ship just drifts. People who have no goals in life just drift.

But if the captain of the ship has a destination, he can have the crew set the sails to make use of any wind, even a wind blowing in the opposite direction. Unfortunately, many people have little idea of what they can achieve in life, and thus they aim at nothing. They feel frustrated, and their confidence is low.

Many people have a difficult time choosing a goal for themselves. This can lead to frustration and low self-confidence.

Suppose you are driving down a highway when you suddenly see a very attractive person in the lane next to you. If you shift your focus to the person in the other car, you will begin to swerve in that direction. You go where you focus your attention.

Remember the six-foot plank? If you focused on crossing the plank, you'd have no trouble. If you focused on the ten-story drop, you could easily fall. Where you send your attention is where you send yourself.

Ask yourself:

- Do I have any goals?
- How specific are they?
- What do I want to be doing a year from now?
- What do I need to do to reach my goal a year from now?
- What do I want to be doing five years from now?

If you think it is farfetched to plan ahead five years, remember, "No wind favors a ship without a destination." If you don't consider where you want to be in five years, you could just drift for five years and end up wherever the winds of life blow you. Then you will feel frustrated. That is no way to build confidence.

Look at the successful people in life. They have something most other people don't have. It's not money, cars, possessions, or big houses, although they may have all those things. They got where

Writing down your goals is the first step in achieving them.

they are because they had goals, and they kept
their goals in sight all the time. They manufactured their confidence by knowing where they
wanted to go, and then they did what it took to get
there. Talk to some of the people in your own life
whom you consider successful. Maybe they can
point you in the right direction.

Changing Can't to Can

A confident person does not believe in **can't**.
Suppose President John F. Kennedy had allowed
can't to control the space program. In 1960, when
he announced his goal to have an American on the

moon within ten years, manned space flight was considered pure science fiction. The scientific community said it was impossible.

"Why is it impossible?" he asked. "Because we don't have the metal, the fuel, and the technology," they responded. He told them to get the metal, the fuel, and the technology. **Can't** was changed to **can**, and on July 20, 1969, the first man set foot on the moon.

Going Step by Step

When you find out the specific reasons why you **can't**, you have actually identified the ways you **can**. You know the steps that make it possible to do what you thought was impossible. Instead of viewing a seemingly impossible goal as one huge job, you break the job down into its parts and then do each part step by step.

Here are the steps in building your confidence:

Set Goals. Set specific, realistic goals that are in keeping with your talents and skills. Obviously a five-foot person would not set a goal of becoming a basketball star, but this person might set a goal of becoming an excellent coach or referee. Identify your own strengths and weaknesses when setting your goals.

• **Having a Goal Brings About the Means.** Once you decide to do something, the means to do it start to show up. When you decide to buy a particular make of car, suddenly you begin to see that car all over the highway and ads for it everywhere. The cars and the ads were there before, but you just didn't notice them. Now you do because you have a goal.

- **Mistakes Are Stepping-Stones.** Instead of viewing mistakes as setbacks, view them as steps toward your goal. When a baby is learning to walk, it falls down many times but just keeps on adjusting until it takes the successful first step.

- **Expect Success, Not Failure.** People who are truly confident don't focus on mistakes. They notice their successes. By keeping their focus on reaching the goal, they have the confidence to continue until the goal is achieved.

- **Trust Yourself.** A confident person has self-trust. To be confident means to have faith in yourself. If you don't trust yourself, you defeat yourself. Confident people can say, "I'm my own favorite person."

Wise Caution

We do the best we can with the self-talk and self-image that we use. So be careful what you put into your self-talk and self-image. It is wise to be cautious, but being overcautious will defeat you.

All of our behavior—including our fear and

Doing well on a test you've studied for can boost your
confidence.

overcautiousness—has a positive intention: to keep
us alive and happy. But sometimes people do
things that can make them miserable, like taking
drugs, drinking habitually, and misusing sex,
because they have decided that they don't like
themselves very much. They fail to realize that
what they're doing is not in keeping with the goal
of life and happiness. Trust yourself and focus on
your positive intentions.

What Are You Doing?

Ask yourself: If I know my goals, what am I
doing to achieve them? Is it working?

Sometimes people set goals but never check whether what they are doing is furthering their goals. If what you have been doing is not producing the results you want, ask yourself a very important question: What can I do differently to reach my goals?

Since you create your own behavior, you can change your behavior. You've surely heard the old saw, "If at first you don't succeed, try, try again." Let's change it to, "If at first you don't succeed, do something else." That doesn't mean that you abandon your goal. It means that you abandon the self-defeating behavior that was not moving you toward the goal.

Winners and Losers

We are all born to win. But we can create "loser" behavior that prevents us from becoming all we were meant to be. Recognizing the "loser" frame of mind can prevent you from behaving like a "loser."

Here is the way a "loser" looks at life:

- **Expects failure.**
- Feels great **anxiety** or even **panic** about life because he or she has little or no sense of control.
- **Imagines dangers and obstacles** everywhere and freezes up.
- Senses **little or no meaning or purpose** in

life and **gives up easily** when goals are not attained.
- Has only a **vague idea of goals** and does not really expect to attain them.

A confident person rejects such self-defeating thoughts. A confident person uses the winner's frame of mind:

- **Expects success.**
- Senses that he or she is **actively involved** in life and therefore has a **sense of control** over his or her life.
- **Uses wise caution in dealing with real problems** and **stays in control of his or her thoughts.**
- Senses that there is **meaning** in life and so **does not give up** when goals are not attained.
- **Keeps working at attaining goals** because he or she expects to attain them eventually.

A "loser" automatically becomes a victim. A victim views himself or herself as an object, a thing that is at the mercy of powerful forces beyond his or her control. But a human being is not designed to be an object. A human being is meant to be a winner. A winner views himself or herself as a responsible person.

Being responsible means being "able to respond" or free to choose. How do you choose to think and act?

Working toward a goal, such as eating healthier foods, can give you a sense of achievement.

Commit yourself to create do-able, realistic, positive goals, and then move toward them step by step.

Commit yourself to stop listening to your negative self-talk or the negative talk of other people. Let other people live their lives, make their choices. You are choosing a new plan and making a commitment to improve your life.

Do It Now

Now is the time to make your commitment.

Many people live in the past and keep reliving all their mistakes and negative experiences. Thus they miss the opportunity to create something new **NOW**. Of course you must learn from the past, but you mustn't keep thinking about it and recreating it. Move ahead and get on with your life.

Now is the only time that Malcolm can decide to go out for the basketball team; that Annette can stop fretting and learn her lines for the play; that Jamal and Tanisha can start talking to each other; that Barb can start eating properly and exercising; that Pedro can acknowledge his real talent; that Angela can see herself as already having everything she needs to be happy; that Nathon can make a good speech to his club; and that Kandace can stop worrying about what other people think of her and start being herself. Whatever they do is up to each one of them.

What are you waiting for? **Now** is the only time that you can put your new plan into effect.

Chapter 5

The New Confident You

Ⅰf you see yourself as a meaningless person leading a purposeless life, you will not be able to manufacture confidence.

Meaning and Purpose in Your Life

Dr. Viktor Frankl was imprisoned in a Nazi concentration camp during World War II. In his book about his experiences, *Man's Search for Meaning*, he writes that the prisoners who gave up on themselves and lost their will to live also lost any sense of meaning in their lives. They were not able to go on, and they died.

The prisoners who did not lose the will to live kept focused on the idea that their lives had purpose. No matter how sick and frail they became, they were alive when the Allied armies liberated the camps. If they could do this in a

Create a mental image of yourself enjoying success.

brutal concentration camp where they faced death every moment of every day, you can do the same no matter what you have to face in your daily life.

Many people do not like what they see when they look in a mirror. Try thinking of yourself this way: "There is only one me in all of human history. I am here for a reason. I have a talent that the world needs. If I don't develop my talent, the world will never have it. I need to become everything I was meant to be. I am here for a reason."

A self-reliant person who has self-esteem can

overcome any problem and accomplish whatever that person needs in life. On the other hand, a person who has no self-trust, no self-worth, no reason for living, will give up at the first sign of trouble. Which kind of person do you choose to be?

Creating New Self-Talk

Replace the old, negative self-talk with new, positive self-talk that will build your new self-confidence.

Positive self-talk has four qualities:

- **It's Personal**. Since your negative thoughts are about **you**, you must talk directly to yourself with your new self-talk. Use "I" in your new belief statements.

Malcolm has been telling himself, "I probably would mess up if I tried to shoot a basket. I'd look silly. Everyone would think I was a jerk." You can hear his negative beliefs about himself.

Listen to how different Malcolm sounds now: "I've been shooting baskets for years. I can do it. I'll show everybody what a good player I am." Does this mean he will make every basket? No. But he's there on the court shooting baskets and feeling confident in his true ability.

- **It's in the Present Tense**. Use self-talk about today, not about the past or the future. The past exists only as lessons you can remember. The future, by definition, never arrives. Speak about your new goals as if they were here with you now. Use present-tense verbs.

Annette has been telling herself, "I'll mess up. I'll forget my lines. I'll be nervous." It's no accident that what she expects to happen does happen.

Instead, Annette now tells herself, "I can learn these lines. I've learned all sorts of things. I've got this down cold. I am doing what it takes to be ready for my performance."

- **It's Positive**. You get what you focus on, so **focus on what you want,** not on what you don't want.

Jamal and Tanisha were both thinking, "I'm not good enough. I'd never be able to say that I'd like to go out on a date. Even if I tried, I'd mess up." They were focused on what they didn't want rather than what they did want.

Their self-talk is different now: "I'm saying how I feel. I want to go out, and it's time to talk about it."

- **It's Powerful**. Do you tell yourself, "I'm an idiot! I'll never succeed! I'm a failure!"? These are strong statements. Make your new self-talk equally powerful in a positive way, showing how much fun you are having aiming at your new goals.

Keep your goal in mind as you strive to achieve it.

Barb has been telling herself, "I just can't do anything to change the fact that I've inherited a heavy body. I can't tell people that I'm trying to eat better and exercise. They'd laugh at me." These are strong statements that express weakness. We can be very powerful in sabotaging ourselves.

Barb now tells herself, "I feel totally great about deciding to lose weight. I'm excited about creating a healthy body with a fantastic good diet and awesome workouts! I love building a new body!"

Thought Reversal

Your mind cannot believe two opposite thoughts at the same time. You can short-circuit negative thoughts by replacing them with positive ones. In psychology this is called "thought reversal."

Think of the worst horror movie you ever saw. Think of how grim and scary it was. Remember every detail that you can and really concentrate on them. Notice what is happening to your thoughts and feelings as you do this.

Now erase that idea. Think of a beautiful spring day in a meadow. See the warm light of the sun on the green grass. Look at the bright colors of all the new flowers. Smell the fresh air and listen to the birds. Notice what is happening to your thoughts and feelings now.

The horror movie scene and the pleasant spring meadow exist only in your mind, but both create powerful feelings and emotions. Wherever your thoughts go, your energy goes. You can create negative energy or positive energy. It all depends on what thoughts you choose.

Be Ready for Your Doubts

In the past you've invested lots of time in making your negative self-talk come true. Don't be surprised now when the old thoughts pop up. Be ready when your mind raises doubts.

Pedro is now telling himself, "I'm jamming at

Accepting occasional self-doubt and moving on enables you to keep working toward your goal.

the keys of my piano, and the band sounds great." Nathon is telling himself, "I'm a good speaker, and I'll be a shoo-in to win the election." Then in the back of their minds they hear doubts. Pedro hears, "Yeah, but suppose you're off-key." Nathon hears, "Yeah, but suppose you forget part of your speech."

These doubts are normal. They're part of your caution. But be ready to counteract these doubts so that you don't become overcautious. Tell yourself, "That's what's so. So what? Now what?"

Let's see why this three-part statement is a powerful cure for doubts:

"That's what's so." Most people lose

confidence because they are afraid that something might go wrong. Telling yourself, "That's what's so" allows you to accept the truth that you are not perfect and that mistakes can happen.

"**So what?**" The question takes away the heavy mental burden that keeps so many people worried. You accept the truth that things might not go the way you planned. Mistakes are stepping-stones toward success.

"**Now what?**" This question refocuses you on the present moment. You can choose new behavior right now. Every new moment gives you the opportunity to make new choices.

And remember, change takes time. Be patient with yourself.

The Seeds of Happiness

Why is Angela frustrated when the new stereo and hairstyle don't make her happy? Because she is looking outside herself for happiness. Happiness comes from the way **you** look at yourself and life, not from the things and people outside.

In an ancient Greek myth, Zeus called an emergency meeting of all the gods on Mount Olympus. He told them, "The humans have spoiled or destroyed every gift we have given them. The only thing left is this bag containing the seeds of happiness. Where can we hide it until humans are wise enough to make good use of the seeds?" The gods pondered the question a long time. At last they hit upon the one place where the seeds would be safe: inside the human heart.

To find happiness, you must accept yourself and become everything you are meant to be. Happiness comes from the way you think and the way you do things. It does not come from outside. It comes from within.

People lose faith in themselves because they think happiness comes from controlling other people. But the only person you can control is yourself. An old saying expresses this idea: "Change the sail, not the wind." As we navigate through life, we cannot control the wind, but we can control how we deal with the wind.

Do You Want to Be Miserable?

The misery that comes from low self-confidence allows us to play victim. When we play victim, we can manipulate other people by gaining their sympathy. We can also excuse ourselves for everything we do because, after all, we tell ourselves that we have no control over our lives.

Is this the way you want to live? Stop being miserable. Choose to rebuild your confidence now. Taking full responsibility for your life may be a bit scary at first. But it's also very exciting once you begin to see the results you can achieve.

Trying a new hobby can help you discover that you have unique skills.

Chapter 6

Aiming for Excellence

Y ou are not perfect, so you don't have to aim at perfection. Aim at excellence. When you are excellent, you make full use of your abilities and you regard yourself as a worthwhile human being. In the excellent frame of mind, you focus on the solution instead of the problem. Excellence brings quality into your life by riveting your attention on your goals instead of on any obstacles in the way.

Volunteering, joining a club, or even taking up a new hobby can be ways of getting more control over your life and gaining a sense of accomplishment.

What Is Failure?

When you aim for excellence, you realize that you cannot succeed without sometimes failing. Most people view failure as a dead end. But failure is important information in disguise. Failure tells you what not to do. The baby learning to walk fails many times, but every failure brings the baby one step closer to success.

Don't define "failure" as disaster resulting from the inability to succeed. Think of it this way:

- Failure is essential to success.
- You cannot succeed without failing often enough to discover what you need to succeed.
- Failure is the process of gathering information, adjusting your course of action, fine tuning, and focusing.
- No great success was ever achieved without all the necessary steps first being taken.
- These steps are commonly called failures.

Hitting the Bull's-Eye

The reason that many smokers lose confidence when they try to quit smoking is that they "fail" the first time, and so they give up. Actually people who do quit smoking "fail" six or seven times before they finally reach their goal. Wealthy people usually "fail" ten or twenty times in various businesses before they reach success.

Giving up after a few "failures" is like trying to hit a bull's-eye the first time. It is unrealistic to expect to be on target immediately. You have to "fail" a number of times to succeed. By "failing,"

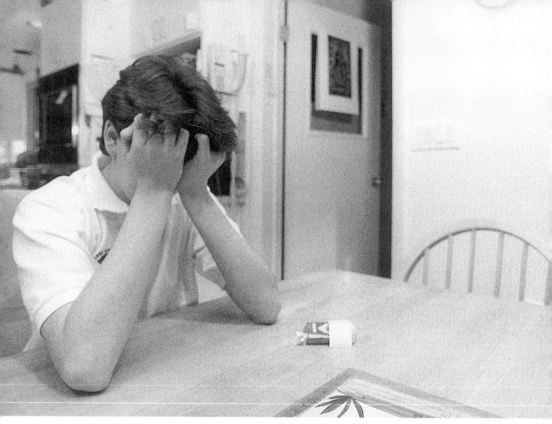

Don't let failure discourage you. Failure is part of the process of achieving success.

you discover ways that don't work. You go step by step toward the way that does work. This is how you aim for excellence.

Your Magic Sword

An old fable illustrates how confidence and failure work. A young knight wanted to be a hero by slaying the dragons that menaced his land. One day he found a sword that glowed strangely. He thought it was a magic sword. He went out and killed a dragon with the sword, and everyone cheered him. He killed another dragon and was praised as a mighty warrior. He killed a third

Believing in yourself is half the battle in achieving a goal.

dragon, a fourth, a fifth, and so on. But then one day an old man told him that the sword was really a piece of scrap metal that had been thrown away by another knight years ago. That day the young knight went out to kill a dragon, but he never came back.

The power was not in the sword. The power was in himself. When he thought the sword had lost its magic, he lost his magic. The only magic involved was the magic he was manufacturing within himself.

The Magic Within You

Let's look at some people who realized that the magic was in themselves.

Demosthenes was an ancient Greek who had a speech defect. He knew that he had something important to tell the people. Day after day he went to the shore, stuffed pebbles in his mouth, and practiced speaking till he could make his voice heard clearly over the sound of the waves. Eventually he became a great Athenian statesman because he was such an eloquent speaker. He aimed at excellence and had confidence in himself.

Although he was partly deaf and had only three months of formal schooling, **Thomas Edison** became the greatest inventor of all time, patenting more than 1,000 inventions. He experimented thousands of times before he found the secret of the electric light. Even though people laughed at him, he knew that each "failure" was a step toward success. He knew he could create the incandescent bulb, and he did. Edison said, "Genius is 1 percent inspiration and 99 percent perspiration." He realized that he could not just wait for things to happen; he had to make them happen. He aimed at excellence and had confidence in himself.

At the age of two, **Helen Keller** had a serious illness that caused her to become blind, deaf, and unable to speak. Almost everyone thought she would go through life never being able to communicate. But her teacher, Anne Sullivan, never gave up. Eventually Helen learned to read, speak, and write. She became a highly educated woman who wrote many books and helped others who seemed beyond help. Her motto was, "The only way out is through," meaning that you cannot solve problems by running away from them. You have to deal with them head-on. Helen Keller and Anne Sullivan both aimed at excellence and had confidence in themselves and in each other.

Greg Louganis was diagnosed as dyslexic, was put up for adoption, felt unwanted and unloved, realized that he was gay, and abandoned himself to drugs and alcohol. But eventually he turned his life around and became such a skilled diver that he competed at the Olympic Games twice and was known as "The World's Greatest Diver." An example of his confidence occurred when he scraped his scalp on the edge of a diving board when performing during the Olympics. He had seen another diver die in a similar incident. But he simply had his scalp stitched and bandaged, got back on the diving board, and made a gold-medal dive. Later, no longer afraid of what people would think of him, he came out publicly and stated that he had AIDS. He helped raise money for AIDS research. He aimed at excellence and had confidence in himself.

These are people just like you. If they can build up their own confidence, so can you.

Many people can help you to build your self-confidence.

Fear and Excitement

When you feel fear, you are experiencing a strong emotion that has a powerful effect on your body. The same is true when you feel excitement. Most people consider fear and excitement very different experiences. But when you aim at excellence, you know that they are the same thing.

Let's see how Malcolm and Annette deal with what they used to call fear.

When Malcolm thinks about basketball or works out with the team, he now tells himself, "Go for it, man!" He pictures himself slam-dunking as the whole gym cheers him on. When he makes a basket, he says, "Smokin'!" When he doesn't make a basket, he tells himself, "OK. Next time." His fear is gone.

Failure does not mean you are defeated. Remember that even walking was once a challenge.

As Annette memorizes her lines for the play, she relaxes and focuses on a mental movie of herself saying the lines on stage in front of a full audience. She tells herself, "I'm giving the best performance of my life." If she actually does make a mistake, she tells herself, "Take a breath and relax. Now on with the show!" She is excited about being in the play.

Situations that used to cause fear now cause excitement. Why? Not because the situations have changed, but because Malcolm and Annette are **doing** and **thinking** differently.

Have Patience with Yourself

Creating your confidence is a lifelong, full-time project. It's exciting to discover who you are and what you are capable of doing. Don't think you are alone in your self-building project. Many people can help you—your family, friends, teachers, and fellow workers.

You have nothing to lose but your old negative thinking. You will gain more of who you really are.

Have patience with yourself. Even though you are not perfect, you can be excellent. You are a valuable human being who is in the process of becoming everything you were meant to be.

Glossary—*Explaining New Words*

alienate To cause a person to become unfriendly or hostile.

caution Forethought and prudence to reduce the risk of danger.

erroneous Mistaken; containing errors.

focus To concentrate one's attention upon an object or subject.

impoverished Poor; deprived of strength or richness.

judgmental Having a tendency to judge harshly.

prophecy Prediction of something to come.

sabotage An act or process designed to hurt or hamper.

Where to Get Help

You can talk about building your confidence with any responsible adult that you trust. You might want to try a family member, a teacher, a social worker, your family doctor, or your family minister, priest, or rabbi.

If you don't feel comfortable talking with any of these people, look in the yellow pages of your telephone book under these listings:

Clergy
Counseling, Personal and Family
Counseling, Human Relations
Human Services Organizations
Mental Health Centers
Psychologists
Physicians and Surgeons
Social Services Organizations
Social Workers
Youth Organizations and Centers

You can also write or call the following U.S. organizations for further assistance:
Big Brothers/Big Sisters of America
230 North 13th Street
Philadelphia, PA 19107

(215) 567-7000

Boys and Girls Clubs of America
771 First Avenue
New York NY 10017
(212) 351-5900

National Mental Health Association
1021 Prince Street
Alexandria, VA 22314-2971
703-684-7722
1-800-433-5959

National Self-Help Clearinghouse
City University of New York
25 West 43rd Street
New York, NY 10036
(212) 354-8525

IN CANADA:

The Self-Help Resource Centre of Greater
   Toronto
40 Orchard View Blvd.
Suite 219
Toronto, Ontario M4R 1B9
(416) 487-4355

For Further Reading

Anthony, Robert. *The Ultimate Secrets of Total Self-Confidence*. New York: Berkeley Books, 1984.

Butler, Pamela. *Self-Assertion for Women*. San Francisco: Harper, 1992.

Frankl, Viktor. *Man's Search for Meaning*. New York: Pocket Books, 1963.

Glasser, William. *Reality Therapy*. New York: Harper & Row, 1975.

Jeffers, Susan. *Feel the Fear and Do It Anyway*. New York: Fawcett Columbine, 1987.

McFarland, Rhoda. *Coping Through Self-Esteem*, rev. ed. New York: The Rosen Publishing Group, 1993.

McWilliams, John-Roger and Peter. *Do It! Let's Get Off Our Butts*. Los Angeles: Prelude, 1991.

Waitley, Denis. *The Psychology of Winning*. New York: Berkley, 1984.

Index

About the Author
Matthew Ignoffo is a college-prep teacher. He has
written many articles and several books. He has master's
and doctoral degrees in English, American Literature, and
Reading Improvement from Loyola University of Chicago,
Northwestern University, and Monmouth College. He is
certified in Neurolinguistics, Hypnotherapy, and Reality
Therapy. In addition to teaching and writing, he counsels
people about self-improvement.

Photo Credits
Cover photo by Michael Brandt; Kim Sonsky (p. 17, 19, 21,
25); Katie McClancy (p. 14, 30); Michael Brandt (p. 53,
56); Lauren Piperno (p. 52, 7); Katherine Hsu (p. 2) Yung-
Hee Chia (all other photos)